ATLAS OF THE EARTH

Illustrated by Daniel Moignot
Produced by Gallimard Jeunesse
and Jean-Pierre Verdet

A FIRST DISCOVERY BOOK

SCHOLASTIC INC.
New York   Toronto   London   Auckland   Sydney

About four billion years ago,
Earth was a ball of burning rock and gases.

About two hundred million years ago,
Earth was made up of a huge ocean
and a huge land mass.

Then, slowly, the land mass split apart into continents.
Today, the continents are drifting as much as several
inches every year.

This map shows different vegetation all over the world.

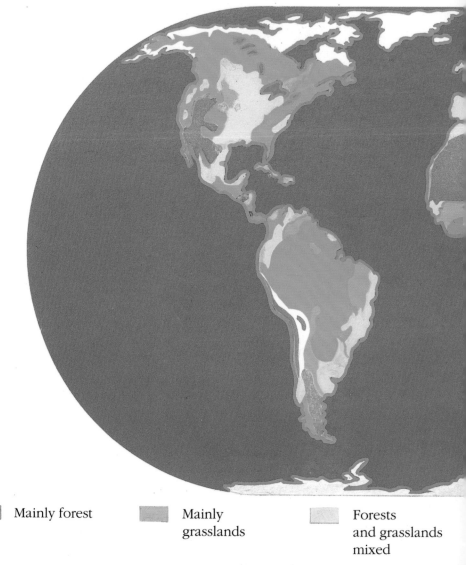

Mainly forest

Mainly grasslands

Forests and grasslands mixed

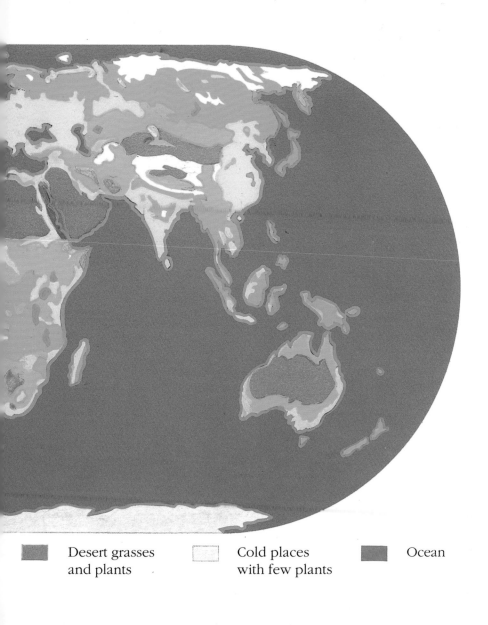

Desert grasses and plants   Cold places with few plants   Ocean

Two-thirds of the Earth is covered
with oceans and seas.

The ocean floor has a surface
as interesting as the surface
of the land.

There are plains, hills,
valleys, and mountains
underwater!

The water is fresh and cool
in this mountain lake.

All rivers, streams, and most lakes
contain freshwater. Some lakes contain saltwater.
Seas and oceans are always saltwater.

The water in the Dead Sea contains much more salt than
the water in the oceans. Fish cannot live in the Dead Sea
because there is too much salt in the water.

Fjords are narrow, deep
valleys that have been
flooded by the ocean.
They were originally
made by glaciers.

Seas can be surrounded by beaches
of sand or by mountains.

More than 500 active volcanoes
exist on land.

Under water, even more
exist on the ocean floor.

Volcanic eruptions spew
molten lava, which
cools and forms
islands.

In parts of North America and Europe, the climate is mild and the land was once covered by forest. Now much of the land has been cleared so that crops can grow in the rich soil.

The steppes of Asia and the pampas of South America
are vast plains that are grassy, but too dry for farming.
The land is good for raising cattle.

Some mountain ranges, such as the Alps,
are only a few million years old.
The wind and the snow have not yet
worn them away.

Other mountains
are many millions
of years old.

Time, wind, and weather
have softened their shapes
and surfaces.

One hundred million years ago,
the Colorado River was a stream
calmly floating along a vast plain.

Then, slowly, the land rose. Instead of quietly crossing a flat plain, the Colorado became a river running down a steep slope. The force of its current dug away at the rock for millions of years and created the Grand Canyon.

In Africa, grassy prairies stretch as far as the eye can see.
These are savannas where herds of zebras graze and roam free.
The weather is always hot, and sometimes wet, too.

Where it almost never rains . . .

The Sahara is a desert so dry that few animals
can live there. In some parts of the Sahara,
it doesn't rain for several years.

The North Pole is on the north polar ice cap.
The Arctic Ocean is very cold.
Inuit hunters live there and fish near the ice.

Birds, polar bears, foxes, seals,
walruses, and whales are
also found there.

The South Pole is located in Antarctica,
the coldest place in the world.

The only people who live there
are scientists who study
the climate. But the sea is teeming
with life. Penguins, whales, and seals make
their home in Antarctica.

Discover some surprising facts!

North Africa has the hottest
temperature records.

The Atacama Desert in Chile
holds the record for dryness.

The coldest place on Earth
is Antarctica. The temperature
can descend to -110° F.
In the winter, the sun doesn't
rise for several months. In the
summer, "white" nights pass
when the sun never sets.

The rainy season
in Northeast India lasts
from June to November.
During that time it can rain
up to 400 inches.

The largest canyon
measures one mile deep
and more than 217 miles long.
It's the Grand Canyon!

The Sahara
is the largest desert
on Earth.

Library of Congress Cataloging-in-Publication Data available.

Originally published in France under the title *Atlas de la Terre* by Editions Gallimard Jeunesse.

ISBN 0-590-96211-6

12 11 10 9 8 7 6 5 4 3 2 1   7 8 9/9 0 1 2/0

Printed in Italy by Editoriale Libraria

First Scholastic printing, August 1997